Southwest Writers Series
General Editor: James W. Lee

21

Alice Corbin Henderson

BY T. M. PEARCE
The University of New Mexico

52894

STECK-VAUGHN COMPANY   AUSTIN, TEXAS

T. M. Pearce has lived in the Southwest for more than forty years. After completing his baccalaureate degree at the University of Montana in 1923, he became a teaching assistant at the University of Pittsburgh, where he was granted an M.A. in 1925 and a Ph.D. in 1930. In the period between the last two degrees, he spent two years, 1927-29, in Albuquerque as an assistant professor of English at the University of New Mexico. So persuasive was the artistic and academic environment in the Southwest that he returned to the University of New Mexico in the fall of 1930 and has remained there ever since. He became Professor-Emeritus of English in 1964. Dr. Pearce has written or contributed to the editing of ten books and has published numerous articles in both academic and non-academic journals.

ACKNOWLEDGMENT

Poems of Alice Corbin are reprinted with the permission of Henry Rago, editor of Poetry, A Magazine of Verse, and of Alice Henderson Rossin, who holds the copyright permissions for her mother's books. Mrs. Rossin supplied books and manuscripts from "The Alice Corbin Henderson Collection" now at El Cuervo Ranch, Tesuque, New Mexico. Without her help and encouragement this study could not have been completed.

Alice Corbin Henderson

Alice Corbin Henderson

Many readers today feel that poetry is a lost art. Verses seem to be written to escape form rather than to establish it, and words appear to conceal meaning rather than to express it. Many readers call for more clarity and for more esthetic discipline. Yet when these same readers look back to the scene of poetry fifty years ago, they discover a similar outcry by critics then, who were puzzled by what was called the "New Poetry" beginning to appear in print or to be recited wherever people gathered to hear a reading. Among the leaders of this new movement in America were Vachel Lindsay, Carl Sandburg, William Vaughn Moody, Amy Lowell, Ezra Pound, Witter Bynner, Arthur Davison Ficke, Hilda Doolittle (better known as "H.D."), and two women who collaborated in editing a magazine of verse called *Poetry*. These two coeditors were Harriet Monroe, founder and editor-in-chief of the magazine when the first issue appeared in October of 1912, and Alice Corbin Henderson, assistant editor from September of that same year until three and a half years later, when failing health required her to give up most of her editorial tasks. Her name then appeared as associate editor until 1922.

Lindsay, Sandburg, Moody, and Monroe lived in Illinois; Lowell in Massachusetts; Pound was originally from Idaho, although he had won fame in England by the time he became a Foreign Correspondent for *Poetry*. Witter Bynner was a New Yorker and Arthur Ficke lived in Iowa. "H.D." was a Pennsylvanian. Alice Corbin was born in Missouri, but lived in Chicago both before and after the new magazine sprang into life. "Sprang" is not a well-chosen word, for Harriet Monroe describes the beginning of her publication as requiring weeks in the Chicago Public Library, where she read the poetry of all contemporary British and American

1

poets and then started to knock on the doors of wealthy Chicagoans to find the money to publish her magazine.

A front room in a large Victorian house at 543 Cass Street (now North Wabash Avenue) was the original home of Miss Monroe's venture, and there behind a large rolltop desk she undertook her first editorial chores. Before she arranged the first table of contents for *Poetry*, she sought the advice of Alice Corbin Henderson, whom she invited to use the second borrowed desk, next to her own. Their editorial office had a noncommercial atmosphere; the files and other furnishings were on each side of a fireplace with a white marble mantel and the added splendor of a gilt-framed mirror and a French marble clock. Parlor chairs casually arranged on a Wilton carpet gave the decor of a studio. The aura was more like a reception room than an office for commercial transactions.

At this time Alice Corbin Henderson was living in the community of Lake Bluff, a Chicago suburb to the north. Her husband, William Penhallow Henderson, had a studio there on land which had been given to Alice by a cousin, Major S. H. Richardson. Since Henderson was teaching at the Chicago Academy of Fine Arts, he also had a studio in the city with living quarters as well as work rooms. This combination of home and shop was in the Tree Studio Building at 10 East Ohio Street. The building was two stories high and provided quarters for four artists; an inner courtyard furnished light and privacy for painters and their models. The Tree studios were not far from the office of *Poetry* magazine, and the proximity of artists to writers stimulated the activities of both groups. The sensitivity of a painter's eye to light and color can be detected in the work of many of the self-styled "New Poets," who associated themselves with the school of writing called Imagism. Both the creed and the practices of this group were a novelty in the early issues of *Poetry*. However, the early work of Alice Corbin Henderson, like the beginning poetry of nearly all the other poets who were publishing before 1912, was not Imagistic in form, but imitative of stanzas and themes which had dominated nineteenth-century English and American poetry. What else was to be found in the schools and colleges at the beginning of the twentieth century?

As a child, Alice Corbin sat in the elementary grades of schools in Illinois, Missouri, and Virginia. She was born in St. Louis on April 16, 1881, but she moved from that city when her mother died of tuberculosis in 1884. That began what was the pilgrimage of her early years. She was sent to Chicago in 1885 to stay with the Richardsons at Lake Bluff. In 1891 her father remarried, and young Alice joined the new family in Kansas City. Two years later she was in Bloomington, Indiana, with her stepmother, who later took Alice back to Kansas City. In 1895 she was sent again to be with the Richardsons in Chicago. Alice entered Hyde Park High School there and was graduated four years later.

The standard poems studied everywhere in the elementary grades were pleasant selections about nature and children's lives written by such New England poets as Longfellow, Whittier, and Lowell. Wordsworth and Tennyson provided romantic lyrics, and Browning supplied faith and optimism in verse at higher scholastic levels. The facts that fifty thousand employees of the Pullman Company were discharged by Chicago owners in 1894 and that troops were sent by President Cleveland to support the Company did not disturb the standard reading programs for literature in the schools, although Vachel Lindsay later wrote his famous poem "The Eagle That Is Forgotten" about Governor Altgeld and his sympathy for the strikers at this time.

American poets in the 1890's created books with such titles as *Blooms of the Berry, Red Leaves and Roses, A Roadside Harp, A Handful of Lavender, The Harvest Moon, Winter Holiday,* and *Songs from Vagabondia.* The last title suggests a path of adventure for the reader as the poet takes him sailing the Seven Seas and tasting the pleasures of the wanderer. None of these voyages stresses the hazards or the grimy side of the sailor's lot. The joyous or melancholy moods of nature, the harmonies of music, the mystery of the moon and stars, the simple pleasures of everyday experience, plus homespun sentiment for the sufferings of life— these were the subjective paths of personal poetic exploration in the youth of Alice Corbin. Rarely did the minor lyricists approach the surge of Walt Whitman or the cryptic condensation of Emily Dickinson. It was the flow of popular-verse writing which surrounded Alice when she prepared her first book of poems and named it *Linnet Songs*. The volume was published in her third year at Hyde Park High School, where Harriet C. Brainard (who later married the poet-dramatist William Vaughn Moody) was her English teacher. Alice had spent the summer at the plantation-type estate of her father's family near Norfolk, Virginia, where she had found opportunity to reflect upon the seventeen years of her life, and the reflections appear in sonnets or in stanzas of three and four lines varying in meter and rhyme. There are also "A Ballade" and ten long lines of rhyming couplets called "A Prayer." Fifty copies of the booklet were printed by the Wind-Tryst Press for Christmas of 1898.

Although she treats such subjects as solitude and snow in a somewhat conventional manner, the sonnet written about John Milton exhibits a vigor of thought that is more than just solemn tribute to a great poet. While praising Milton's majestic lines and concepts, the young Chicago poetess also measures the limitations of his century and of the audience which he addressed:

MILTON

O mind bound down by earthly similes
And harassed by conceptions of your time,
With what intense, receptive joy we seize
Your vast ideas fettered by no rhyme,
And surging with majestic sweep of sound!
Hampered for years by human narrowness,
At last you had your cherished project crowned
With merited, magnificent success.
And though all due applause we give to you,
Yet when your soul finds immortality,
And in our great creation's plan you trace
No streets of gold, nor any compass true,
You'll know that All-embracing Whole is free
From limit of all sound, or time, or place.

Although the seventeen poems in *Linnet Songs* are imitative of models popular in the academic curriculum, they are skillfully molded, and they explore some avenues of thought which were to persist throughout Alice Corbin's writing career. "Let my senses be stirred by experience" is her theme in one poem, and in another

4

she states, "I choose to suffer pain, if that is the price of happiness." The number of seventeen poems in the first book of a seventeen-year-old girl was an original idea whether suggested by the poetess or her advisor at the Press. Perhaps the cousin Alice Richardson, to whom the book is dedicated, proposed the number and also chose the antique type with decorative initial letters which set off the first line of each poem. Fourteen years were to elapse before Alice Corbin would publish a second book.

Alice entered the University of Chicago in the fall of 1899 at the urging of Miss Brainard, whose home was a meeting place for the literati of the city. Alice lived with her during these years at the University, but after suffering from chest inflammation in the winter of 1902 she went south to enter Sophie Newcomb College in New Orleans. This was the homeland of her mother's family, the Carradines, and Alice spent her summer with relatives at Ocean Springs and Biloxi, Mississippi. A girl who had lived seventeen of her twenty-one years in Illinois or Missouri was likely to view the conservative social customs of the Old South with restrained amusement. While enrolled at Sophie Newcomb, Alice found a position as book reviewer for the New Orleans *Times-Picayune*, an association with the world of journalism which was highly rewarding from her literary point of view. However, Madame Detreuil, teacher of Alice's course in English literature, viewed such contact with the crudities of newspaper circles with deep suspicion. She devoted the greater part of her lectures to advice about how the young ladies should deport themselves outside academic precincts, spicing this guidance with literary reminiscences of her own life in London society.

"I didn't know then," wrote Alice Corbin Henderson many years later, "that Walt Whitman and Lafcadio Hearn had served apprentice days on New Orleans newspapers, or I might have been awed by my own aspirations." Professional experience in journalism was an asset when Alice returned to Chicago in the fall of 1903. She began to write reviews for the Chicago *Tribune* and the *Evening Post*. The following year, she rented a studio at the Academy of Fine Arts. There she met William Penhallow Henderson, an art instructor from Boston. He had just returned from two years of study in Europe, where his travels had introduced him to the works of Cezanne, Van Gogh, Renoir, Manet, Whistler, Rembrandt, and other great painters. The artist and the young journalist-poet were caught up in the swirl of a cultural renaissance in Chicago. Art, music, ballet, drama, and literature were flourishing. Isadora Duncan, having first introduced her revolutionary dance programs to Chicago audiences, returned in 1905 from triumphs in Europe. Pavlova and Nijinsky also played a season in that year. The great Bernhardt intoned French classic theater, and a local playwright named William Vaughn Moody won success with a drama called *The Great Divide*. Caruso, a new tenor, appeared at the opera house as did Farrar, Nordica, and other great artists. The sculptor Lorado Taft, the cartoonist George Barr McCutcheon, and the satirist and novelist Henry B. Fuller were also adding luster to the Chicago group at this time.

William P. Henderson had left the Academy in the summer of 1904 for a sketching trip to Mexico and Arizona. He brought back pictures of the Grand Canyon and the Hopi Indian villages which recorded the splendor of Southwestern landscapes and the life of minority population groups as colorful tapestries on the edge of America's mainstream. He and Alice Corbin were married on October 14, 1905, establishing their home at Lake Bluff and retaining Henderson's studio in Chicago. When Alice Corbin became Mrs. W. P. Henderson she continued to use her maiden name in signing her poems. She used her married name as a writer of prose. As Alice Corbin Henderson she became the editor of two books to which Alice Corbin contributed poems. She gave up her work in the city when her daughter Alice Oliver was born on January 27, 1907. During the time of her pregnancy she had been writing plays for children, the plots of which were adapted from the Biblical stories of the Creation, the Nativity, and the Resurrection of Jesus. Henderson collaborated with his wife by illustrating the plays with woodcuts. He also made the colored lithographs for her next book, which was a translation entitled *Andersen's Best Fairy Tales*. The collection includes such famed stories as "The Emperor's New Clothes," "The Little Match Girl,"

"The Ugly Duckling," and "The Tin Soldier." From the financial returns of this book came a trip to Europe, beginning in July of 1910. They took their daughter with them to visit Italy, France, Spain, and Holland. The family returned in September, 1911, with new projects for the horizon in Chicago.

Alice had a second book of poems for her publisher. William Henderson had many European sketches to place on canvas for exhibition and to use in lectures at the Academy. Furthermore, lively currents of poetry were stirring in the Chicago literary whirl, along with rumors of the new magazine as a publishing outlet. It is probably far from coincidence that when her new book *The Spinning Woman of the Sky* appeared in December, 1912, four of its best poems also appeared in that month's issue of *Poetry* magazine. Scanning these four poems and comparing their form and development with others, the reader is led to believe that had Alice Corbin Henderson been longer in her editorial role, she would have written a different book. *The Spinning Woman of the Sky* is a more mature work than *Linnet Songs*, but the poet has not yet found her distinctive voice nor her authentic idiom. She has thirty-three poems in the book, of which twelve are devoted to the earth, sea, sky, moon, and stars; eight to symbols and moods such as the harp, lyre, cup, silver balls, and shadowy visions; five to classic themes suggested by the Vale of Arcady, Pygmalion, Daphnis, and Adonis; three to objects of beauty in art such as Rodin's statue of Eve; and five to religious subjects, the modern world, and the idea of progress expressed in weapons and mechanical power. The four poems which appear in both the magazine and the book illustrate a capacity for compression and emphasis upon sensory impression which are two of the elements stressed by the Imagist School. Quotations will illustrate these qualities better than they can be defined:

THE STAR
I saw a star fall in the night,
And a grey moth touched my cheek;
Such majesty immortals have.
Such pity for the weak.

Who was it built the cradle wrought of gold?
A druid chanting by the waters old.
Who was it kept the sword of vision bright?
A warrior, falling darkly in the fight.
Who was it put the crown upon the dove?
A woman, paling in the arms of love.
Oh, who but these, since Adam ceased to be,
Have kept their ancient guard about the Tree?

"Falling stars" and "moth" become images of mortality in the endless life stream; the "cradle," "sword," and the "dove" symbolize the covenant of religion, power through war, and the pledge of love. After six months of publishing the poems of Imagists, the editors of *Poetry* decided to present the guidelines for poets who desired to join the school of Imagism. Chosen to present these rules and procedures were two of the practitioners, F. S. Flint and Ezra Pound. Flint was an Englishman and a student of the French Symbolists Verlaine, Baudelaire, and Mallarmé. Pound was an American iconoclast, hostile to the verbose rhetorical elegance of nineteenth-century poetry in English and determined to reestablish poetry on more realistic and objective grounds. They stated the Imagist creed in *Poetry* for March 1913 (Vol. I, No. 6). Flint declared that the Imagists were not a "revolutionary school," but a group returning to the classic principles of writing poetry as exemplified by Sappho, Catullus, and the medieval François Villon. The Imagists were intolerant of the dilettantism they found prevalent in literary circles, and they insisted upon the direct treatment of poetic experience, free from decorative embellishment. They advocated strict economy in presentation and urged free rhythmic lines. All verses should be rewritten until the maximum of compression reached a perfection of organic form.

Ezra Pound had called the American public a "mass of dolts" in the first poem he sent to *Poetry*. He entitled this poem "To Whistler, American," and then wrote lines in which he praised Whistler as a nonconformist, like himself, who experimented constantly amid uncertainties, but succeeded, as Lincoln did, despite public opposition. Miss Monroe had to defend Pound against the protests from readers who objected to being called "dolts." She chose, therefore, to point out in February of 1913 that Mr. Pound was not the first American poet who had been forced to leave America because of indifference to his work. Her support must have encouraged Pound to expand upon Flint's brief article with a manifesto which he called "A Few Don'ts by an Imagiste." Pound goes to the essence of the new outlook by defining "Image" at greater length. He writes that an "Image" is an impression which "presents an intellectual and emotional complex in an instant of time." He then explains that he is using the term "complex" in the technical sense employed by newer psychologists, implying a system of desires plus memories which exert a dominating influence upon personality. Pound states that from this poetic principle comes "that sense of freedom from time limits and space limits; that sense of sudden growth, which we experience in the presence of the greatest works of art. It is better to present one Image in a lifetime than to produce voluminous works." Having completed such positive emphasis, Pound then goes on to add a dozen or more proscriptions for men and women who intend to write poetry, such as:

Ignore the criticism of those who have never themselves written a notable work.

Use no superfluous word, no adjective, which does not reveal something.

Use either good ornament or no ornament at all.

Don't imagine a thing will "go" in verse just because it is too dull to go in prose.

Don't be descriptive; remember that a painter can describe a landscape much better than you can.

Don't chop your lines into separate iambs and make them start and stop within the line unit, but catch the rise of the rhythm wave and move it to a conclusion logical to the thought.

These lessons on how to become an Imagist were not so simple as they may sound. Pound was trying to establish critical standards in order to distinguish good verse from bad in terms of clear-cut observation, vivid diction, and significant associations of meaning with imagery. All good poetry will stand the test of such criteria.

One of the Chicago journalists-turned-poet, or perhaps one of the poets-turned-journalist, was Carl Sandburg, son of an immigrant Swedish railroad worker. As a young man Sandburg felt poetry as experience when he worked as a scene shifter in the theater or listened to the word pictures of William Jennings Bryan, who in 1894 came to Galesburg, Illinois, when Carl was sixteen years old. In this same year Carl first visited Chicago, borrowing his father's railroad pass to take him to the city for a visit as long as the money would last. He added to his store of imagery when he rode a box-car to Fort Madison, Iowa, crossing the Mississippi for the first time. Sandburg worked his way as far west as Denver, washing dishes, selling hot tamales, pitching wheat in Kansas. He kept a journal of these travels and wrote down "word exercises."

Carl Sandburg enrolled as a freshman in Lombard College the same year that Alice Corbin entered the University of Chicago, although he was three years her senior. He participated fully in the life of his college and remained long enough to earn a baccalaureate degree. In 1904 he published a small book of twenty-two poems entitled *In Reckless Ecstasy*. Although uneven in quality, these were strangely like the verses of the mature Sandburg which Alice Corbin Henderson presented to Harriet Monroe twelve years later for *Poetry*. Miss Monroe described them as "a group of strange poems in very individual free verse, beginning with 'Chicago' as the 'hog-butcher of the world.'" The two editors gave the nine poems a featured position in their magazine for March 1914 and therewith provoked a controversy heard in orthodox circles of poetry throughout the world. The uproar made both the magazine and Sandburg famous.

Miss Monroe's word-portrait of Alice as she enlivened the editorial office for three and a half years deserves quotation: "Her round face with its smiling Cupid mouth, blue eyes, and impertinent little nose, never prepared one for the sharp wit which would flash out like a sword. She was a pitiless reader of manuscripts; nothing stodgy or imitative would get by her finely sifting intelligence, and we had many a secret laugh over the confessional 'hot stuff' or the boggy word weeds which tender-minded authors apparently mistook for poetry." In Alice's copy of the book in which this description appears (A *Poet's Life*) the word "blue" is encircled in pencil and "BROWN!" written as annotation.

Monroe and Henderson published other poems by Sandburg in May and November, and then in October 1915 the magazine printed seventeen short lyrics in which Sandburg demonstrated that his range of feeling and observation was broader than just city streets, the market, or even the lake front, harbor, and music hall. These new sketches produced poetry about loneliness, a harvest moon, the rain, the sun, and a human face. These were in the group of poems which Alice Corbin Henderson took with her in the autumn to New York and left with Alfred Harcourt, a salesman for Henry Holt and Company. In the following spring, *Chicago Poems* by Carl Sandburg appeared under the Holt imprint, as did another book of his, *Cornhuskers*, two years later. After Alfred Harcourt established his own publishing house, Sandburg sent him manuscripts for nearly fifty years, including poems, songs, reminiscences, stories, and the six-volume set of Abraham Lincoln's biography. No more lasting and satisfactory publishing relationship seems ever to have been recorded. Perhaps Alice sensed this when she became the contact between Sandburg, Harcourt, and a reading public.

Carl and Alice remained friends throughout her lifetime. On January 8, 1915, he sent her a letter containing the following excerpt:

Dear A. C. H.: —

I have sent to Mr. Harcourt some 260 poems, each one neatly typed or pasted on a sheet by itself, all of it paged, and headed by an index, and table of contents under the title "Chicago Poems." I wanted much to have you go over them before they went on but he sent me two letters about the stuff, I am away behind in sleep, and work, and for peace of soul I had to get the whole thing out of the house and off my mind. As you were the original "discoverer" of the "Chicago Poems," and evocator of that title, and as it was you who told Harcourt *et al.* these poems were worth going after, your suggestions on what should have gone into the bunch would have been worthwhile . . . . You would have

been a proper personage to be present at the launching ceremony to pronounce prophecies as the bottle was broken on
the prow . . . .

CARL SANDBURG

In the letter just quoted Sandburg wrote a postscript in which
he referred to poems by Alice which had appeared in the January
issue of *Poetry*. He called them "lovely and finished things" and
remarked that "it is a blasphemous shame that publishers and
public insist on bulk in books of poetry, that the call is for big
multitudinous Lorado Taft Marches of Time rather than Paul
Manship bronzes." His comparison of size and volume in art is
pertinent to Alice Corbin Henderson as an artist, for her four
books of poetry contain fewer poems than Sandburg placed in his
first book. His field of operations spread to the four corners of
the land. Alice Corbin Henderson surveyed the earth and sky
from fewer points of vantage, but her look was searching and her
concentration intense.

In December 1915 Sandburg wrote Alice that he and Edgar
Lee Masters, another Chicagoan, were planning to have Lake
Bluff moved closer to the loop so that they could see her more
often. He called both Alice and Harriet Monroe "Modern Forces"
and concluded with the statement: "Coiled inside the graphite
of my pencil (is) also a disquisition on your poetry and your personal urge for the brief and poignant." Harriet Monroe testifies
that Alice Corbin Henderson was also responsible for *Poetry's*
discovery of Edgar Lee Masters, who, during his career as a lawyer,
had written and published several small books of academic verse
under various pseudonyms before he published fragments of his
Spoon River Anthology. He was using the pen name of "Webster
Ford" when he sent one of these fragments to the St. Louis *Mirror,*
where Alice saw it. She wrote to the author, and he sent her
additional poems which she printed in the October 1914 *Poetry*
editorial column called "Our Contemporaries." The complete
book of poems in the *Spoon River Anthology* was published the
following year. At an "Editors' Night" held by the Book and Play
Club in February, Masters told how encouragement by the editors
of *Poetry* furnished the spark which kindled his mind to complete

the anthology. When both *Chicago Poems* and *Spoon River Anthology* were ready for notices in *Poetry*, they were sent to Alice Corbin Henderson for reviewing, but she was too ill to carry on her work. The success of Sandburg and Masters had confirmed her judgment and strengthened her conviction that poetry would move in new directions in the United States.

After Alice recovered her health at Sunmount Sanatorium, Sandburg and Vachel Lindsay came to Santa Fe for public readings of their poetry and for a reunion with her. Others from the Chicago circle, Masters and Harriet Monroe among them, were drawn, as if by a magnet, to a new poetic center established in the Southwest. Santa Fe became no exile for the former associate editor of *Poetry*, since she continued to contribute to the magazine and her literary associates did not abandon her. The environment she had established followed her to Santa Fe. Through her presence there, poetry in New Mexico developed a maturity it had not known before.

The Henderson family had arrived in the capital city of New Mexico on March 18, 1916, and the first order of business had been to find Alice the necessary rest and medical care. They chose a sanatorium southeast of the city and named Sunmount because it was near a mountain by that name. There Alice Corbin Henderson found others like herself, exiled from places in the East and South, with an illness like her own. Morale is almost as important as physical factors in the cure of tuberculosis. She wrote to Carl Sandburg on March 28 thanking him for some clippings and notes which he had sent and stating that she found the country "simply glorious." From her cottage she could look across the "sand-combed valley to the west—with mesas rising out of it—and blue and purple around some snow-capped mountains of the Sangre de Cristo range beyond." Carl replied on April 2 that many people were inquiring about her and that his answer was that she had "slipped into quiet, pearl-walled caves of quiet, and was learning new values of dream."

The famous poet of India, Rabindranath Tagore, had been welcomed in early numbers of *Poetry* and by the editors themselves when he came to Chicago in 1912 and again in 1913. After a lecture at Baylor University in January 1917, he invited the Hendersons to meet him at Lamy, New Mexico, the railroad stop for Santa Fe. The station was near a charming Fred Harvey hotel, with a handsome lounge built from the old vigas of an abandoned mission. There, before the glow of piñon logs in a huge fireplace, the poet read from his play "King of the Dark Night." Tagore had invited them for the stopover without realizing that the station for passengers entering Santa Fe was twenty miles from the city!

Robert Frost wrote to the editors of *Poetry* on November 2, 1917, thanking them for the Prize Award of one hundred dollars for his poem "Snow." In this letter he confides, "it is my first real prize in a long life. Hitherto my utmost had been a few dollars for running at a Caledonia Club Picnic; a part interest in a pair of ear-rings, and a part interest in a gold-headed cane for impersonations at a masquerade; a gold medal for shear [sic] goodness in a high school; and a Detur for scholarship at Harvard." When this acknowledgment was received, Alice Henderson had left the sanatorium and was living with her family in a small house just inside the city limits. The street was then called Telephone Road, because the poles and lines were conspicuous. Alice appeared before the City Council and asked them to restore the street's old name, which had been *El Camino del Monte Sol,* or Road of the Sun Mountain. When the petition was granted, she and her daughter bought the street sign and nailed it up from horseback.

One of the big events of the literary world of 1917 was the appearance in February of *The New Poetry, An Anthology,* which Harriet Monroe and Alice Corbin Henderson had been preparing throughout the previous year. In the book were selections from the work of one hundred and one poets, chiefly English and American. As Miss Monroe explains in her "Introduction," all the poems had been written within the last seventeen years. Each was chosen because it bore some relationship to the progressive modern movement, a movement toward greater freedom of form and spirit, including some radical endeavors in the "ever-conquering spirit of beauty." There were such poems as "Irradiations" by John Gould Fletcher, "Images" by Richard Aldington, "Chinoiseries" by Amy Lowell, and "Cinquains" by Adelaide Crapsey. Wilfred W. Gibson

14

offered his dramatic anti-war monologues in verse. D. H. Lawrence probed beneath the surface of nature and man to forge rhythms for words, and Ezra Pound spoke the complexity of his thoughts in English, Greek, French, Italian, and even translations from the Chinese. "Anthology," as a Greek word, means, in its literal sense, "a collection of flowers," but accompanying the glow of imagery and fragrance suggested by poems like Tagore's "The Garden," Upward's "The Marigold," and Frost's "After Apple Picking" were the inquests and analyses found in Bodenheim's "The Rear Porches of an Apartment Building," Hagedorn's "Broadway," Corbin's "One City Only," Hardy's "The Man He Killed," and Sandburg's "Our Prayer of Thanks." One poem that represented a mood neither warmly glowing nor sternly probing was called "Portrait of a Lady." The author was T. S. Eliot. He chose a form which combined rhymed with unrhymed lines, modulating them in length and rhythm. His attitude was detached, almost tentative and noncommittal. The poem tested the air for a new sophistication in literature, one that would sweep a rising generation into an attitude of gentle skepticism and ironic disdain.

The anthology included a group which was largely idealistic. These poets compared this world to a better one that could be conceived with help from the imagination. The members wrote as though they believed such a world to have some reality. All majestic, romantic, dreaming, exuberant, mystical, and optimistic writers share this subjective attitude, and, if the anthology can be considered a representative selection of poets, such writers were in the majority in 1917. Frost, Sandburg, and Lindsay can be chosen as three notable representatives of the idealistic line. By comparison, there was a skeptical group of empirical writers who related the actual to the factual and evaluated what they observed as deficiencies in men and society. They wrote objectively, and their frank appraisals anticipated a world of better understanding. Eliot's "Portrait of a Lady," Masters' "Silence," and Stevens' "Peter Quince at the Clavier" inaugurated a list of prospective empiricals. To be exact in finding labels for literary movements or fixing their limits is difficult, but perhaps 1912 to 1922 marks the period when the idealistic group was dominant among the New Poets, and

15

1922 to 1932 covers the conquest by the empiricals, who have also been called "metaphysicals," a perplexing term because it implies "philosophic disciplines" and requires considerable explanation. Ezra Pound became a bridge between the two schools, since he tried to reconstruct the idealistic tradition and to a large degree became empirical. D. H. Lawrence, on the other hand, was empirical from the start but never ceased to be exuberantly idealistic.

Alice Corbin Henderson contributed ten poems to the anthology, nine of which had appeared in *Poetry* between 1912 and 1916; the tenth had appeared in *The Spinning Woman of the Sky*. Two short poems are quoted below to illustrate the impact of what Sandburg meant when he referred to Alice's "urge for the brief and poignant." She was an idealist in her statements even when they involved pain and grief.

APPARITIONS

I

A thin gray shadow on the edge of thought
Hiding its wounds:
These are the wounds of sorrow —
It was my hand that made them;
And this gray shadow that resembles you
Is my own heart, weeping . . .
You sleep quietly beneath the shade
Of willows in the south.

I I

When the cold dawn stood above the house-tops,
Too late I remembered the cry
In the night of a wild bird flying
Through the rain-filled sky.

LOVE ME AT LAST

Love me at last, or if you will not,
  Leave me;
Hard words could never, as these half-words,
  Grieve me:
Love me at last—or leave me.

Love me at last, or let the last word uttered
  Be but your own;
Love me, or leave me—as a cloud, a vapor,
  Or a bird flown.
Love me at last—I am but sliding water
  Over a stone.

For a woman who had been ill, Alice Henderson staged a re-markable return to vitality. In February 1917 she participated with four other poets in what might be called a "Symposium on Abo-riginal Verse." The rostrum was still *Poetry* magazine, and the master of ceremonies was Harriet Monroe, who referred in her "Editorial Comment" to the poems which were motivated by American-Indian sources as "mines of folklore" embodying racial feeling and rhythm. She said that the approach to this literature was by way of both science and art, because scientists in the U. S. Bureau of Ethnology and other scientific institutions have supplied transcriptions to which the poets have given artistic form. In some rare individuals the literary and scientific gifts were combined; this was true of Frank Cushing, who translated the "Creation Myth" and *Zuñi Folk Tales*. Natalie Curtis also combined research with creative skill in *The Indian's Book*, as did Alice C. Fletcher in her study of the songs and festivals of various tribes. At Miss Monroe's request, a second "Editorial Comment" was supplied by Carl Sand-burg, who paid tribute to the wealth of Indian oral literature by reproducing four of Miss Frances Densmore's transcriptions of Indian poetry. He concluded from the specimens that "the Red Man and his children committed direct plagiarisms on the modern imagists and vorticists." Alice Corbin Henderson was the third editorial commentator, and she explained how in her *Indian Songs* she took the keynote of a translation, which was often just a single image or phrase, and expanded it slightly. The Indian song was usually accompanied by pantomime and gesture. She tried to supply some of this missing framework of action by filling in with her own words what the Indian words failed to convey. She said that in every case she tried to keep within the spirit of the Indian originals.

The *Indian Songs* to which she referred are a drama in seven

17

poetic parts. The first poem, "Listening," presents in four lines the setting of a prairie where the silence is broken by the noise of passing feet. In "Buffalo Dance" the thunder of hooves and the tossing of curved horns become action in the scene. "Where the Fight Was" tells how a man dies in battle. "The Wind" describes the spirit of the dead warrior whirling around the sky. "Courtship" relates that the dead warrior offers gifts to persuade his wife to join him in the place of departed ones. "Fear" asks her to mourn in the spirit of companionship with the dead, and "Parting" speaks of reunion after death. Only one of the seven short epigrams need be quoted to convey the impact of each segment of this tragic cycle.

PARTING

Now I go, do not weep, woman —
Woman, do not weep;
Though I go from you to die,
We shall both lie down
At the foot of the hill, and sleep.
Now I go, do not weep, woman —
Woman, do not weep;
Earth is our mother and our tent the sky.
Though I go from you to die,
We shall both lie down
At the foot of the hill, and sleep.

The other poets in the symposium upon aboriginal American verse are Frank S. Gordon, a physician who lived in both Mexico and the Southwest; Mary Austin, a writer whose books *The Land of Little Rain* and *The Flock* had established her among the foremost interpreters of both Indian and Spanish peoples; and Constance Lindsay Skinner, who traveled among Indian tribes in Central America and reported folkways in both verse and prose. All seven of these Alice Corbin Henderson poems appeared in *The Path on the Rainbow*, edited by George W. Cronyn in the following year. In the editor's "Acknowledgments" the statement is made that *Poetry* magazine not only inspired the preparation of the book, but also supplied some of its best material.

There was more to think about than poetry in the life of a civic-minded woman with a husband who was painting for art exhibitions in California and a ten-year-old daughter who was trying to "turn cowboy" after learning how to ride horseback in a Western saddle. All the Hendersons enjoyed visiting the Indian pueblos on ceremonial days when the chorus sang and the Summer and Winter people danced for good harvest and good hunting. After the United States entered World War I on April 6, 1917, there was less time for such visits, as Alice Henderson became Publicity Chairman for the Woman's Auxiliary of the State Board of Defense. In the following year, William Henderson went to California to employ his painting skill as a camoufleur for the Navy in the shipyards of San Francisco. His family spent part of the year with him.

Poets from the East and Midwest were beginning to include Santa Fe on their Western tours, sometimes when they were scheduled to read their poetry and at other times when they simply planned to discuss poetry with Alice Corbin Henderson. Vachel Lindsay arrived to lecture in the fall of 1919 and again in 1921. On March 25, 1921, Carl Sandburg telegraphed Alice as follows: "Indefatigable Tireless Troubadour Troops attack Lamy nine seven Saturday Morning. (signed) Lief the Lucky." He spoke to Santa Fe audiences several times during the 1920's and the 1930's. Robert Frost spoke and visited in Santa Fe. John Gould Fletcher, Bliss Carman, and Arthur Davison Ficke stayed at various times in the city. In 1921 a former acquaintance of the Chicago days, the poet Witter Bynner, wrote to Alice inquiring about a place to recuperate from an attack of influenza. She recommended the sanatorium where she had regained her health. He stayed there six weeks and then bought a house, which he renovated, enlarged, and made into a museum of art objects acquired in China during the period when he prepared *The Jade Mountain*. This book of verse was an adaptation in English of three hundred short poems written by Chinese soldiers, scholars, monks, emperors and empresses, young people and old, philosophers and statesmen—poets all—during the period 618-906 A. D.

There had been hints in her contributions to *Poetry* after she left Chicago that Alice Corbin Henderson was finding new themes for her writing in the Southwestern environment. Perhaps she little realized when she began to write about the brilliant sunlight, the brown hills, the windswept canyons, and the exotic flowers, plants, and animals in the arid Southwest that she was creating a poetic vocabulary and forming new concepts of time where geology lay naked to the view. A primitive people still lived in ancient dwellings with a way of life bound to the earth and the sky by incantations and gestures filled with religious meaning and drama. A European group, older than any other in the United States, retained many of their folk arts and folk customs preserved from the Hispanic heritage to which they belonged. These folk traditions enriched the poetry in Alice Corbin Henderson's third book, which she called *Red Earth, Poems of New Mexico*. The volume contained fifty-seven poems, all of which had been written between 1912 and the date of publication in December 1920. Fourteen of the poems were inspired by Spanish-American motifs or themes; twelve were suggested by Indian life or ceremony; thirty-one were contemporary Anglo-American responses to a region as non-English in soil, sky, humidity, temperature, flora and fauna as New Mexico, which had been an early historic title for all of the American West. The book was published in Chicago. Though not the first book of poetry about the Southwest, it was perhaps the most original, since the author created a Southwestern poetic idiom to explore a new spectrum of imagery. As a poet she made an Anglo-Saxon reading public live awhile in the world of the Pueblo Indians, and she transferred these readers inside the memory of a venerable old Mexican woman recapturing her youth. One of her poems portrays a sheepherder who has lived so long in solitude that his mind has begun to turn, and the people say that a boy will take his place in the coming year. In these poems Spanish terms find their way into American-English poetry as casually as they had been adopted by the people who spoke them in the region. A little river is a "rito," a ditch an "acequia," and a pine a "piñon" when it can find the type font to give it a Spanish spelling.

In May of 1917 Alice Henderson had reviewed *Wild Earth and Other Poems* by Padraic Colum, whom she called "one of the most gifted, if not the most gifted, of the younger poets." In the course of her review, she refers to William Butler Yeats as the old veteran of the Celtic renaissance in Irish poetry. He was the first of the Irish poets to express the primitive understanding of life which makes culture possible. Such depth of feeling is eliminated where modern efficiency and system sterilize folk experience, as has happened in dominant nations today. The title *Red Earth* in 1920 is like another banner beside Padraic Colum's *Wild Earth*, each announcing that the place where a people live is a manifesto of their strength and assets.

Harriet Monroe in her "Introduction" to *The New Poetry* reports that when Yeats spoke in Chicago he criticized Victorian poetry as too formal and remote from life. The Irish poets wanted to get away from the academic refinement and elegance which separated poetry from the simplicity of basic feeling. They wanted to strip poetry of its artificial diction, to achieve a style closer to speech and sound "like a cry of the heart," Yeats said. This vision of the field of poetry was in the mind of Alice Corbin Henderson as she contemplated the Southwest in her day, a day of beginnings for expressing the inspiration behind Indian, Spanish, and Anglo-American patterns of life. This may sound like anthropology in verse, but whatever anthropology or sociology Alice learned became word rhythms, music, and portraiture before she was finished with it. In *Red Earth* she found a new and authentic voice as a poet, not an Indian voice nor a Spanish voice nor an Anglo voice, but a personal voice expressing the lives of the peoples among whom she lived and interpreting their experiences and her own in the immediacy of regional color and speech.

In her "Notes" to *Red Earth*, she wrote that poetry to the Indians was not description but a mirror of the nature in which they lived and worshiped. The words and gestures had a reality much more direct than anything on a printed page. They were dramatic in the most realistic sense, because the words made images and symbols which produced an emotional response. She offers the following poem as a representation of a ceremony in verse:

THE GREEN CORN DANCE

San Ildefonso

Far in the east
The gods beat
On thunder drums. . .

With rhythmic thud
The dancers' feet
Answer the beat
Of the thunder drums.

Eagle feather
On raven hair,
With bright tablita's
Turquoise glare.

Tasselled corn
Stands tall and fair
From rain-washed roots
Through lambent air.

Corn springs up
From the seed in the ground,
The cradled corn
By the sun is found.

Eagle feather
And turkey plume
From the wind-swept cloud
Bring rain and gloom.

Hid in the cloud
The wind brings rain
And the water-song
To the dust-parched plain.

Far in the east
The gods retreat
As the thunder drums
Grow small and sweet.

The dancers' feet
Echo the sound
As the drums grow faint
And the rain comes down.

Two shorter poems from *Red Earth* achieve the image previously defined by Ezra Pound as being "an intellectual and emotional complex in an instant of time."

GOLD

Gold is under these hills;
And the wind piles sand
Through the cracks of deserted cabins.
Gold chinked over the counters,
Gold poured into the glasses,
Gold flickered and flamed
In the spendthrift gleam
Of a woman's hair . . .
Gold is under these hills,
Gold in the empty sunlight.

FAME

Fame is an echo
Far off, remote —
But love is a sweetness
You taste in the throat,
Friendship a comfort
When twilight falls.
But fame is an echo
Through empty halls.

The poet became ill again in the spring of 1921. Vachel Lindsay stopped at Sunmount for a visit. According to Witter Bynner, Alice soon recovered enough to brew coffee and hold court for a few friends, some of them poets. Among the visitors was a cowboy-poet, N. Howard ("Jack") Thorp, the first collector of songs of the range, which he published in a small paperback book printed at Estancia, New Mexico, in 1908. It contained twenty-four song-poems, five of which Thorp had written, despite the mistaken

23

modesty which led him to disavow the fact in his "Preface." The most important of Thorp's compositions was "Little Joe, the Wrangler," a text which he wrote on an old paper bag using a pencil stub while he sat beside a campfire on a trail drive in 1898. The ballad is about a young horse wrangler from Texas, who left his home because his father remarried and his stepmother beat him. He joined a cattle outfit and was assigned to work with the remuda, but when a thunderstorm caused the cattle to stampede, Little Joe was called out to ride with the cowboys. Trying to check the leaders in their speed, the Texas wrangler fell into a water draw and was crushed to death under his horse. The story is true, and the melody for which the words were written is "The Little Old Log Cabin in the Lane," a frontier tune which is plaintive but not mournful. Of all the Western ballads, "Little Joe, the Wrangler" is one of the half dozen most often sung. Because of Thorp's careless disclaimer, he was never able to establish ownership of the ballad, and he lost all claim to the profits from sheet music, disc recordings, radio broadcasting, and other rights. Verse rarely becomes very profitable, but this Western folk-ballad was known throughout the range country. The song was commercially profitable, but none of the money ever reached the composer.

When "Jack" Thorp arranged his *Songs of the Cowboys* for an edition by the Houghton Mifflin Company in 1921, he asked Alice Henderson to write an "Introduction" to the anthology which had now grown to a total of one hundred and one poems. In this larger collection, Thorp signed twenty-seven of the songs as his own compositions. He identified the other songs by authors or by someone who sang them and the place he heard them sung. In some instances the singer was a cowboy, in others a medicine vendor or a cowgirl who joined the men at roundup. This careful documentation leads Alice Henderson in her "Introduction" to discuss the origins of ballads, whether of English, Scotch, or American traditions. Her remarks are an expansion of what she wrote in an editorial for *Poetry* four years earlier, where she called the cowboy songs America's most indigenous folk poetry with the exception of Negro folk songs. She urged the folklore societies to pay as much attention to them as they did to tracing the survivals of old English or Scotch ballads. She rejects theories that folk ballads must be of anonymous origin and preserved by oral tradition to be authentic, pointing to examples of folk songs by Robert Burns and Stephen Foster which are the heritage of two nations. She asserts that it is the use of a song rather than its origin which determines what is known as folk song. If there is group unity of interest or occupation to insure popularity of a song, plus a certain degree of isolation from a larger world of affairs, the song may pass from one community to another and be handed down from generation to generation. Of course its appeal will depend upon strength of sentiment, story, and language, but the communal audience and isolated situation are fundamental to folk quality.

A careful reader of the 1921 edition of *Songs of the Cowboys* will be interested to find a poem of Alice Corbin Henderson's called "Ten Thousand Texas Rangers," annotated as "Written in March, 1917, at the time when Germany proposed to Mexico that they retake the 'lost provinces' of Texas, New Mexico, Arizona, and California." The date indicates that the friendship between "Jack" Thorp and the author of the poem began shortly after she arrived in Santa Fe. The poem may have been added after she wrote her "Introduction," for she speaks of the "hundred songs that make up this book," whereas the addition of her own poem made the count one hundred and one. A better supposition is that she did not consider "Ten Thousand Texas Rangers" a typical and genuine cowboy song. It may never have found a musical framework, although the rhythm was like that of "Sam Bass" or "The Cowboys' Christmas Ball," and a tune would have been easy to find. The sentiment was tied to the period as the song declares that neither Pancho Villa nor the Rangers had any use for the Kaiser, and the song ends as follows:

> Ten thousand Texas Rangers are shakin' with
>   wicked glee
> At the joke of the German Kaiser in his fierce
>   perplexity;

They are bustin' their buttins with laughin', they
are laughin' fit to kill —
"By Gawd," sez they, "but that's one on him, by
Gawd, but that's one on Bill!"

In 1923 the second edition of *The New Poetry* appeared. Alice
Corbin Henderson was listed as coeditor, and six of her poems
were added to the group. All had been written since she had
moved to Santa Fe and were republished from her volume *Red
Earth* and their initial printing in *Poetry* of February and November 1917. The senior editor, Miss Monroe, remarked that Alice
could give little help with revisions, since her home in Santa Fe
was remote from necessary contacts. New contacts as well as old,
however, made possible an anthology of her own, which Alice arranged for the press in 1928. The title was *The Turquoise Trail,
An Anthology of New Mexico Poetry*. The heading does not read
by New Mexico poets, but of New Mexico poets. Thirty-seven
contributors are represented, only three of whom had been born
in the state. Those three were S. Omar Barker, Margaret (Peggy)
Pond Church, and Eda Lou Walton. Twelve could be called
"residents," or poets domiciled in the state for a considerable
period of time, and they were Mary Austin, Witter Bynner, Alice
Corbin, Paul Horgan, Willard (Spud) Johnson, D. H. Lawrence,
Haniel Long, Mabel Dodge Luhan, Eugene Manlove Rhodes,
Lucy Sturges, N. Howard ("Jack") Thorp, and John Curtis Under-
wood. Ten were "sojourners," whose stay was temporary and who
recorded the impressions of an indweller of limited time. Such
were Willa Cather, Arthur Davison Ficke, John Gould Fletcher,
Marsden Hartley, Henry Herbert Knibbs, Maurice Lesemann, Lynn
Riggs, H. J. Spinden, Glenway Wescott, and Yvor Winters. The
final group were the visitors, whose view was a fleeting one, since
their imaginations were stimulated by brief encounters with what
was either familiar or strange. The fresh, quick report is sometimes the most lasting, as the writing of the following poets may
testify: Badger Clark, John Galsworthy, Alfred Kreymborg, Janet
Lewis, Vachel Lindsay, Harriet Monroe, James Rorty, Carl Sandburg, William Haskell Simpson, Stanley Vestal, and Edith Wyatt.

The unity in *The Turquoise Trail* is found in the stimulus which the locale provided for a creative outlook. In her "Preface" Alice Corbin makes clear that this is the emphasis she intended.

The Turquoise Trail is named for a well-worn trade route from Old Mexico to New Mexico. Over this trail the Indians came north to exchange bright-colored macaw feathers for the sacred blue-green stones of the Pueblos—both of which were used in ceremonial rites. Southwest of Santa Fe, north of Cerrillos, is Turquoise Mountain, where almost a million cubic yards of turquoise stone is believed to have been excavated before the days of the Spanish in the Southwest. *El Camino Real* led to turquoise mines as well as to royal villas and settlements. The title of the book, then, signifies the poetic traditions of the earliest native inhabitants of the region and of the earliest—as well as later— European settlers.

The Turquoise Trail is a collection of poems about a series of happenings. One such happening is the experience of John Gould Fletcher when he first rode horseback up a canyon in which cliff dwellings stood on a shelf of stone; inside the houses were shards of pottery, and outside them the dripping of water became a clock in the centuries of silence. Willa Cather retraces in her memory of history the herds of cattle and sheep being driven by the men of New Spain, and music being played on mandolins beside the water ditches in the evenings. Witter Bynner in "A Dance for Rain" watches the Indians moving in a line before the candles of a shrine:

> Before a saint in a Christian dress
> I saw them dance their holiness,
> I saw them reminding him all day long
> That death is weak and life is strong
> And urging the fertile earth to yield
> Seed from the loin and seed from the field.

D. H. Lawrence tells of autumn at Taos when the rounded slopes of the Rockies appear "like the yellow hair of a tigress brindled with pine." But John Galsworthy, a fellow Englishman, admits in "Desert Song" that he misses the smell of rain. Lynn Riggs takes a "Morning Walk" in Santa Fe and meets four burros on Canyon Road moving like a river of placid hooves. And Willard (Spud) Johnson in "Navaho Legend" recalls that the sun was first carried across the sky by a turquoise man on a blue stallion and that after them came the silver light of day.

Inscribing the book of poems to the authors as a "record of companionships," Alice Henderson wrote: "the covers of the book now take the place of the low-roofed adobe houses within whose walls most of the poems have, at one time or another, been shared in manuscript form." Adobe is sun-dried mud (reinforced by straw) which, when used as a building-block on a stone foundation, can last forever if surfaced with regularity or protected by cement plaster. From 1917 until 1923, the Hendersons lived in a small adobe house near Sunmount Sanatorium, but in 1924 they built a larger place on the Camino near the studio William Penhallow had constructed in 1919. By this later time the road had become a long line of studios and dwellings in the adapted Pueblo Indian architectural style, which called for Navaho rugs and Rio Grande pottery to ornament tables and fireplace shelves. Carved *santos*, or saints, colored over a plaster surface stood in niches cut from the whitewashed walls. The atmosphere of such regional houses was at once formal and charming. In 1922 the Hendersons' daughter, Alice Oliver, married John Evans of Taos, the son of the writer Mabel Dodge Luhan by a former marriage. The young couple built their own home in Tesuque, a village north of Santa Fe. Grandchildren in the years that followed the building of both houses became the occasions for shared companionship within the families and for joint entertainment of friends and acquaintances in Santa Fe, Tesuque, and Taos.

The poems Alice Corbin Henderson contributed to *The Turquoise Trail* had first been printed either in *Red Earth* or a periodical. At the time the anthology appeared, two new projects had begun to occupy her mind. The first was a summer gathering of poets who were living in Santa Fe or who were invited to come there to recite their poetry at a money-raising program for the Southwest Indian Association. Circumstances leading to this annual conclave are interestingly described by Haniel Long, who calls Alice Corbin Henderson "definitely a group person," meaning that she drew people to her because she paid attention to them as individuals. A number of her friends were members of the New Mexico Association on Indian Affairs, and upon one occasion they were meeting in a lovely Santa Fe garden discussing how the Association could raise money. Alice proposed that they sponsor readings by the local poets. Another poet supported the idea, and suggested that a member of the group who was an officer of the Association act as master of ceremonies. This member accepted the invitation and volunteered to wear her cowboy outfit to enliven the occasion. "Then it can be a rodeo," someone prompted, "and the poets can be horses." Alice later recalled that the first of these "Roundups" was held in the same garden on August 16, 1930, and that when Witter Bynner had completed the reading of "A Dance for Rain at Cochiti," the heavens opened and such a downpour fell that the entire audience had to find shelter in the living room, dining room, hall, and porches of the residence. Nevertheless, of the ten Roundups from 1930 to 1939, all but two were held either in gardens or spacious patios, none of which were exactly corrals, but which at least allowed the literary herd a semblance of space.

The various Roundups had among their tame or wild cowboy troubadours such poets as Mary Austin, Lynn Riggs, John Gould Fletcher, Witter Bynner, Haniel Long, Alice Corbin Henderson, Ernest Thompson Seton, Fray Angelico Chavez, William Pillin, Dorothy Belle Flanagan, Josephine Pinckney, Peggy Pond Church, Langdon Mitchell, Joseph Spinden, Stanley Vestal (Walter S. Campbell), Lucy Sturgis, Margaret Lohlker, Ina Sizer Cassidy, and others. At the 1934 poetry reading, held on August 9, E. Dana Johnson, editor of the Santa Fe New Mexican, appeared with flowing black ribbons attached to his glasses. He read from an enormous portfolio labelled "Pomes," which contained an amusing verse satire about the artist colony at Taos. As a serious contribution, he read the epitaph which Eugene Manlove Rhodes had written for himself. Rhodes had died at Pacific Beach, California, on June 27, 1934. In this epitaph Rhodes refers to arising at the sound of the last trumpet, chatting with the angel Gabriel, and then sauntering down the road to hell:

> He will pause loitering at the infernal gate,
> Advising Satan on affairs of state,
> Complaining loudly that the roads are bad
> And bragging what a jolly grave he had!

Because of illness, Mary Austin had been unable to meet with the others for the rehearsal program, but she arrived for the Roundup, reading a series of children's prayers found in her book *The Children Sing in the Far West*. She died at her home in Santa Fe just two days later.

Thornton Wilder had been invited to introduce the participants in the ninth Roundup, and he offered dramatic praise to the poets for their contribution to the contemporary world. At this exhibition of literary skill, the poets read as a benefit for the second project which was consuming much of Alice Corbin Henderson's time. She had helped to organize a regional publishing house called Writers' Editions. Since the Roundups were attended by two hundred or more people, the admission fees of one dollar were a beginning toward the cost of printing small books of verse. The contributions went to Writers' Editions instead of to the fund of the Indian Association. During the poetry series nearly all the performers had made some concession to ranch attire; to complete the background some had chosen Indian and Spanish costumes. However, on one occasion, a Santa Fe woman noted for her independence as well as her literary skills appeared in boots and breeches announcing that she was tired of being a Navaho squaw or a Spanish lady and for once was going to be herself.

At the final Poets' Roundup there was no suggestion of the Western informality that gave the name for the previous occasions. No one sang his songs as Lynn Riggs and Stanley Vestal had done at other meetings. There were no improvised "chutes" out of which the poets were once described as coming, but instead an Olympus-like balcony on which the muses stood. For the first time there was no introduction of visiting poets who, when the Roundup was Western, were called "dark horses." Only seven poets read, and their verses were more satiric and humorous than had usually been the case. The crowd was as large as ever and just as enthusiastic, but the novelty seemed to have worn off and the spirits of the poets were flagging. Of Roundups there were no more.

Writers' Editions, which has just been mentioned, was scarcely an outgrowth of the Roundups, but a number of the same individuals participated in both, something of the same spirit was shown, and the period of activity was nearly the same. Early in 1932 a group of the Santa Fe writers had begun to talk about a kind of publishing guild. Alice Corbin Henderson and Haniel Long, both poets, were active in the group, as was Ray Otis, a novelist. Pivotal to the project was Walter L. Goodwin, Jr., who had brought a press to Santa Fe and had been a member of a similar cooperative type of setup in the East. There was no editor-in-chief or chairman, but an editorial committee voted approval of manuscripts and the author or a sponsor guaranteed the cost rather than sharing in returns on a royalty basis. One of the first Writers' Editions books to appear in 1933 was *The Sun Turns West* by Alice Corbin, the name she always used in signing poetry. The type had been hand-set and the edition printed was limited to five hundred copies. On a front endpaper the statement was made that most of the poems in the volume were written approximately between 1915 and 1932. Two other books by poets appeared the same year: *Atlantides* by Haniel Long and *Foretaste* by Peggy Pond Church. The bindings were in cloth of attractive colors with bright shades of contrast for the letters in the titles. Between 1933 and 1939, fourteen publications came from Writers' Editions, fulfilling the statement which appears on most of the books that this group of writers believed that "regional publication should foster the growth of American literature."

The Sun Turns West is as autobiographical as *Red Earth* is biographical. The first is written by the poet about herself and the second is written by the poet about New Mexico and the Southwest, the people and the places that make both distinctive. The poetry in *Red Earth* is objective. That in *The Sun Turns West* is subjective, beginning with a section (Part I) dealing with Alice

31

Corbin Henderson's memories of her youth. "One City Only" recalls the mellow light of a summer afternoon in Norfolk, Virginia, the water front, the tidal smell, Negro boys jumping from log to log in the harbor, and the recessed windows of the gloomy halls in a big Southern house. "Secret" reveals intimate feelings of a child's pride when an old serving-woman praises her golden hair. "Shadow" describes the fear of a white child when the police hunt for a Negro hiding behind the walls in the white folk's part of town. "Four-o-clocks" is about the child's grandmother and how the ferryboat captain and the bank clerks disregarded the clock when she was delayed for appointments. "Adolescence" expresses the anxiety of a maturing girl made restless by the April air and the fragrance of spring. "Old Houses" is another showcase of memories associated with places in the early life of the poet. The section can be summarized by the final poem:

LIKE A SMALL CHILD

Like a small child bewildered in a place
All bright and new, the world that I have known
Exists no longer, and I stand alone
Frightened by distance I can not retrace:
Oh, we can never quite escape the past!
It comes before us like a sudden flood,
And what has ever entered bone and blood
Is ours and of us till the very last!
Only some stark division makes us feel
The past we live in is the world that's real.

Part II consists of twelve short lyrics called "Songs for a Book of Airs." Each is the mood of a moment—joyous, sad, or serene. The second song becomes a credo for the poet, as positive as she has expressed it anywhere in her writing:

I I

O world that changes under my hand,
    O brown world, bitter and bright,
And full of hidden recesses
    Of love and light—

> O world, what use would there be to me
>> Of power beyond power
> To change or establish new balance,
>> To build, or deflower?
>
> O world, what use would there be?
>> Had I the Creator's fire,
> I could not build you nearer
>> To my heart's desire!

A cryptic humor lies close to the surface in certain of Alice Corbin's short poems. The third of her "Songs" in *The Sun Turns West* illustrates this quality:

III

> A king's but a puppet,
>> A lover a fool,
> A sage is a wise man
>> Who was never at school.
>
> Then why should I bother
>> To read in a book?
> *The world is my fancy*
>> *Wherever I look!*

Humor combines with irony in Part III, which is entitled "Divided Thoughts." Many of the poems are enigmatic. "Unknown Joy" states that happiness is often dependent upon concealed sources, as a pool may be stirred by the wind unseen. "Music" tolls the dirge of sounds no longer remembered. "Monica Silva" is the title which identifies seven sonnets telling the story of a broken friendship. Hurt pride, transient joy, hypocrisy, ghosts of the past, and the solace of beauty are themes to illustrate a friendship that was only a transient bliss. The diction in these sonnets is exquisite, the variety of rhyming in the sestets ingenious, and the story a riddle as stories in sonnet sequences always are.

Part IV, "Another Spring," concludes *The Sun Turns West*. Some sixteen poems are built about the theme of the creative power in life and even in death. Some of the poems record the ecstasy of surging growth in the world of nature. "Flame" registers another type of emotional response, engendered, not by the beauty in nature, but by a human being:

FLAME

Why, when he was not strange to me,
Or different from any other man,
Should suddenly a flame spring up
About him as he ran—
As if a tree within a tree
Had struck up from the root,
And little flames instead of leaves
Were bearing fiery fruit.

In "The Wood" the poet describes the metamorphosis in a landscape which changes from land to sea. At the close of the book there are four sonnets grouped under the heading "Tomorrow Death." Alice Corbin Henderson's thought is that life has continuity with all that precedes and all that follows the personal interim. Her greatest wish has been for that peace which enables one to contemplate a tree or a mountain. Death might offer such tranquil ecstasy. Age views the changes as a means of growth, adding more and more to life. The last sonnet fulfills the thought of the other three.

I V

This love, this beauty, even this love's decay,
Is shadowy substance of some world to be:
I never could think otherwise, or see
How anything that is, can pass away.
If what has happened, happened just to-day,
And not to-morrow, or had never been
Before all yesterdays — how could time spin
The cloth to cloathe the womb, the stone, the clay?

Whatever happens, happened long ago.
Nothing is new; this fluctuating breath,
This love, this pain, this image of quick death
That is not death, though I would have it so,
Is to be borne — to fill some bitter need
Before the sun had ever dropped a seed.

The Sun Turns West is Alice Corbin's finest book of poetry, finished in execution and penetrating in imagination. It is not so pioneering in theme nor so original as Red Earth, but the author is more mature in her craft, richer in thought. Her friend

34

John Gould Fletcher, in a review written for *Poetry* magazine, compares her "Songs for a Book of Airs" to the lyrics of Robert Herrick and the poems in Parts III and IV to the work of Yeats and George Russell ("A. E.") and to the lyrics of James Joyce. Alice was fifty-one years old when she published her fourth and last book of poetry. The title certainly refers to the turning of time, the fading of life's intensity and power. *Red Earth* in 1920 is a living, animated painting of the Southwest; *The Sun Turns West* in 1933 is a living, animated portrait of Alice Corbin Henderson.

Searching for new and unusual types of song led Alice to collect the *alabados*, or Spanish religious songs, of New Mexico, especially those in the hymn books of the Penitentes, a brotherhood of Spanish Americans within the Roman Catholic Church. The society in 1833 was referred to by a visiting bishop from Mexico as *Los Hermanos Penitentes*, "The Penitent Brothers," but in 1934 the group was incorporated with the full title of *La Fraternidad de Jesus Nazareno* (*Los Penitentes*). In the initiation ceremonies which occur on Ash Wednesday, the brethren are called *Los Hermanos de Luz*, or "The Brothers of Light." This is the title which Alice Henderson chose for her book, published in 1937, which contains not only a short history of the society but also a vivid description of the rites and ceremonies of Easter week. Penitents whip themselves and then carry heavy crosses, and one supreme flagellant is tied to a cross in imitation of the crucifixion of Jesus for the sins of the world.

Aside from translations of the songs found in a Penitente copybook, *Brothers of Light* presents a sympathetic story of the charitable activities of the Society throughout the year in administering help and comfort to the families of members. After the Mexican Revolution many isolated communities in New Mexico had no priests, and the native people were left to perform their own rituals for weddings, christenings, or funerals. The *Hermanos Penitentes* assumed these responsibilities. Their prayers and hymns took the nature of folksongs influencing the religious history of the region.

Alice wrote a "Foreword" to another collection of native songs, which had been arranged and transcribed by Mary R. Van Stone in 1928. The title was *Spanish Folksongs of New Mexico*. Though the songs were popular, romantic, patriotic, and humorous, Alice refers to the *alabados*, too, and the part they played in the community spirit. In 1935 she selected verses she had written for her children and grandchildren, calling them *A Child's Bouquet*. Mary Morley set the poems to music. Although the booklet was designed and printed in Chicago, the group of songs carried the publisher's imprint of Writers' Editions, Santa Fe. One of the songs is named "Saying Grace." The lyric mood and charm in statement are typical of the poet:

SAYING GRACE

The silver rain, the singing sun,
The fields where scarlet poppies run,
And all that makes a grain of wheat,
Is in the bread that I do eat.

So when I sit for every meal,
And say a grace, I always feel
That I am eating rain and sun,
And fields where scarlet poppies run.

From July 7, 1936, until July 15, 1937, Alice Henderson served as editor-in-chief for the New Mexico project of the American Guide Series. She wrote the chapter on "Literature," in which she begins the regional story with the myths, legends, and rituals of the Indians as recaptured by anthropologists such as Frank Cushing and Washington Matthews. She reports the written records from the Spanish chronicles of exploration and conquest in the sixteenth and seventeenth centuries. When the Santa Fe Trail opened Mexican territory in 1821, the cycle of written records of exploration and eventual conquest was repeated, but this time written in English. Her essay lists all the significant books on the New Mexico shelf, and occasionally a personal observation indicates that the approach is not entirely bibliographical. Of General Lew Wallace, when he was in charge of the Old Palace from 1878 to 1881, Alice writes that "as territorial governor he divided his attention between Christian gladiators in Rome and the affairs of Billy the Kid in New Mexico." She states that the poets were among the first writers to feel and express the spirit of the country.

After resigning her editorial work for the *New Mexico State Guide*, she accepted the post of librarian and curator for the Museum of Navaho Ceremonial Art in Santa Fe. This building had been designed and constructed by William P. Henderson; consequently, when Alice took the position, the Hendersons were invited to move to the living quarters provided in the building. Not long after Henderson had built his studio in Santa Fe, he had organized a construction firm devoted to the Pueblo-Spanish style. The Navaho Museum, however, was designed like a gigantic mountain hogan, octagonal in shape with a huge entrance facing east and with great windowless walls. The building is unique, as are the reproductions of Navaho sandpaintings and recordings preserved within the museum for visitors.

In 1939 Alice Henderson gave a course of lectures at the Arsuna School and Art Gallery then occupying the Mary Austin house on the Camino del Monte Sol. In the discussions she stressed that the Southwest was still a distinctive cultural province in the United States because the Indian and Spanish cultures were maintained with sufficient strength to modify the Anglo-Saxon tradition. She also said that some American writers were expatriates in Europe seeking a Mediterranean tradition already established by Spanish settlers in the Southwest. During the year 1940 Alice was active in planning for the Coronado Cuarto-Centennial, which was a statewide series of rodeos, fiestas, pageants, and conferences to commemorate the *entrada* of Captain-General Francisco Vásquez de Coronado into New Mexico in the summer of 1540. She wrote an amusing poem called "A Ballade of Historians" which she dedicated to the Committee in charge of the Cuarto-Centennial. This poem was modeled upon the famous poem by François Villon "Ballade of Dead Ladies," with the refrain "Where are the snows of yesteryear?" Alice chose to ask "Where are the Pueblos of yesteryear?" She jested with the historians about their uncertainties:

Where were Senecu and Socorro?
Where Quivira — I'd love to know!
Where, oh where, did De Vaca wander,

In, or out, of New Mexico?
Where was the Red House, Chichilticalli,
Where did Fray Marcos get, how near
To the Seven Cities now known as Zuñi —
WHERE ARE THE PUEBLOS OF YESTERYEAR?

The last nine years of Alice Henderson's life were spent at "El Cuervo," the ranch home of her daughter, Alice H. Rossin. William P. Henderson died suddenly there in 1943, in the home which he had redesigned sixteen years earlier. "El Cuervo" is the Spanish name for "raven," which is also the French word *corbin* found in the surnames of medieval England. After the death of her husband, Alice spent a great deal of time organizing the voluminous files of manuscripts and letters accumulated during her years with *Poetry* magazine, the Poets' Roundup, and Writers' Editions. She worked actively for the Association on American-Indian Affairs, the Indian Arts Fund, the Laboratory of Anthropology, and the Museum of Navaho Ceremonial Art. Writers consulted her for help with their manuscripts. In the fall of 1947 she made a disc recording of six of her favorite poems, reading in soft, expressive tones five poems from *Red Earth* and one from the *New Mexico Quarterly Review*. Through these years she was frequently ill from chest colds and a failing heart. A few weeks before her death on July 18, 1949, she had been honored by tributes from nine of her friends, whose remarks were published in the Spring issue of the *New Mexico Quarterly Review*. The articles were grouped under the heading "Alice Corbin: An Appreciation," and they were edited by Witter Bynner and Oliver La Farge. One of the contributors was George Dillon, who was then, as well as later, an editor of *Poetry* magazine. Dillon had joined the staff as an assistant editor in 1925, and in his article he mentioned how vividly people in the Chicago Little Theatre and the Poetry Club still remembered her. He quotes from letters Alice sent to Miss Monroe in which she made suggestions for the improvement of the magazine, including the exhortation to "Keep *Poetry*, up, up!"

What is "up" as a concept for poetry? Poetic art was probably highest, in one sense, at its beginning, when it was closest to religion; this kind of poetry is found in the "Psalms" of David and the dramas produced by the Greeks before pagan altars. Poetry was then a form of prayer. Later the techniques of poetic expression, such as its rhythmic structure, were adapted to narratives like epics and romances. Poetic forms also came to serve for epigrams, elegies, satires, and didactic pieces. Criticism of such efforts began with Aristotle, who introduced the term *mimesis* or "imitation" as an explanation for poetic motivation. In more modern times, Wordsworth defined poetry as "the spontaneous overflow of powerful feelings," indicating a physiological and psychological compulsion to shape an oral or written composition. A. E. Housman is more casual about his stimulus when he reveals that after drinking a pint of beer at lunch, he frequently went for a walk, and as he looked around him without any particular object in view, a line of verse or a whole stanza would flow into his mind. At the Poets' Roundup in Santa Fe on August 16, 1932, Mary Austin stated that the soothing motion of the Santa Fe Railroad always inspired her to write verse.

What is poetry? To Alice Corbin Henderson it was imagination and compassion. She could be called a "neo-primitive" in her poems about Indians and Spanish life written for *Red Earth*. John Gould Fletcher, in his article for the *Quarterly* "Appreciation," cites her poem "Juan Quintana" as having the quality of folk portrayal found in the poets of the Irish Renaissance:

> The goat-herd follows his flock
> Over the sandy plain,
> And the goats nibble the rabbit-bush
> Acrid with desert rain.
>
> Old Juan Quintana's coat
> Is a faded purple blue,
> And his hat is a warm plum-brown,
> And his trousers a tawny hue.
>
> He is sunburnt like the hills,
> And his eyes have a strange goat look.
> And when I came on him alone,
> He suddenly quivered and shook.

If this is "Imagism," it is the imagery which in 1913 Ezra Pound said was centered around "an intellectual and emotional complex in an instant of time." T. S. Eliot maintained in 1951 that poems were produced by an "objective correlative," which he described as "a set of objects, a situation, a chain of events" evoking a particular emotion. Either statement combines the "imitation" of Aristotle with the "overflow of feelings" identified by Wordsworth. Only the terminology is altered; the ingredients remain the same.

The poem, "Cundiyo," also printed in *Red Earth*, contains the quality of mysticism, compassion, and reality praised as folk portrayal:

> As I came down from Cundiyo,
> Upon the road to Chimayo
>   I met three women walking;
> Each held a sorrow to her breast,
> And one of them a small cross pressed —
>   Three black-shawled women walking.
>
> "Now why is it that you must go
> Up the long road to Cundiyo?"
>   The old one did the talking:
> "I go to bless a dying son."
> "And I a sweetheart never won."
>   Three women slowly walking.
>
> The third one opened wide her shawl
> And showed a new-born baby small
>   That slept without a sorrow:
> "And I, in haste that we be wed —
> Too late, too late, if he be dead!
>   The Padre comes tomorrow."
>
> As I went up to Cundiyo,
> In the grey dawn from Chimayo,
>   I met three women walking;
> And over paths of sand and rocks
> Were men who carried a long box —
>   Beside three women walking.

Since the days of the "Imagists" and the "Empiricals," the outlook of poetry has sought a new language. Whether it is the language of escape or the language of involvment is not clear to many readers. The present-day "New Poets" say they project rather than compose; they release tension rather than emotion;

40

and they measure rhythm in terms of breathing rather than by word stress. Like the Saxon scop or Celtic bard, they call upon musical instruments to frame their readings and direct their sounds. They may even dance their meaning like their tribal forbears. However, they cannot ignore their more immediate predecessors, nor repudiate a line of descent. The "New Poets" of fifty years ago won freedom for American poetry and were the liberators of poets of today. Among these liberators, Alice Corbin Henderson holds a secure place.

Selected Bibliography

BOOKS BY ALICE CORBIN HENDERSON

Adam's Dream and Two Other Miracle Plays for Children (New York: Charles Scribner's Sons, 1909).

Andersen's Best Fairy Tales, illustrated by Wm. P. Henderson (Chicago, New York: Rand McNally and Co., 1911).

Brothers of Light, The Penitentes of the Southwest, illustrated by Wm. P. Henderson (New York: Harcourt, Brace and Co., 1937).

A Child's Bouquet, music by Mary Morley (Santa Fe: Writers' Editions; designed and printed by Ralph Fletcher Seymour, Chicago, 1935).

Linnet Songs (Chicago: Wind-Tryst Press, 1898).

The New Poetry, An Anthology, ed. with Harriet Monroe (New York: The Macmillan Co., 1917, 1923, 1932).

Red Earth (Chicago: Ralph Fletcher Seymour, 1920, 1921).

The Spinning Woman of the Sky, with an original lithograph by Wm. P. Henderson (Chicago: Ralph Fletcher Seymour, 1912).

The Sun Turns West (Santa Fe: Writers' Editions, 1933).

The Turquoise Trail, An Anthology of New Mexico Poetry, ed. Alice Corbin Henderson (Boston and New York: Houghton Mifflin Co., 1928).

SECONDARY SOURCES

BYNNER, WITTER and OLIVER LA FARGE, ed., "Alice Corbin: An Appreciation," *New Mexico Quarterly Review,* XIX (Spring 1949), 34-79. Contains the following essays: "Alice and I," Witter Bynner; "Alice Corbin Henderson and *Poetry,*" George Dillon; "Alice Corbin and Imagism," John Gould Fletcher; "Three Poems," Alice Corbin; "Alice," Carl Sandburg; "Alice Corbin," Padraic Colum; "Santa Fe in the Twenties," Ruth Laughlin; "The Poets' Round-Up," Haniel Long; "The Rabble," Spud Johnson; "The Penitente Book," Oliver La Farge.

The Cambridge History of American Literature, ed. W. P. Trent, John Erskine, Stuart P. Sherman, and Carl Van Doren. In Three Volumes (New York: The Macmillan Co.; Cambridge, England: University Press, 1946).

CARGILL, OSCAR, ed., *The Social Revolt, American Literature from 1888 to 1914* (New York: The Macmillan Co., 1933).

CHAVEZ, FRAY ANGELICO, "The Penitentes of New Mexico," *New Mexico Historical Review,* XXIX (April 1954), 97-123.

CROWDER, RICHARD, *Carl Sandburg* (New York: Twayne Publishers, 1964).

CUNNINGHAM, J. V., "Poetry Chronicle: Envoi, "*Hound and Horn,* VI (Oct.- Dec. 1932), 124-30.

ELIOT, T. S., "Hamlet," in *Selected Essays* (London: Faber and Faber, 1951).

HOUSMAN, A. E., *The Name and Nature of Poetry* (New York: The Macmillan Co.; Cambridge, England: University Press, 1933).

LOMAX, JOHN A., *Adventures of a Ballad Hunter* (New York: The Macmillan Co., 1947).

——————, *Cowboy Songs and Other Frontier Ballads* (New York: Sturgis and Walton, 1910, 1916; with an "Introduction" by Barrett Wendell, The Macmillan Co., 1923; revised and enlarged edition prepared with Alan Lomax, The Macmillan Co., 1945).

LOWELL, AMY, *Some Imagist Poets* (New York: The Macmillan Co., 1915, 1916, 1917).

——————, *Tendencies in Modern American Poetry* (New York: The Macmillan Co., 1917).

MAJOR, MABEL and T. M. PEARCE, ed., *Signature of the Sun, Southwest Verse, 1900-1950* (Albuquerque: University of New Mexico Press, 1950).

MONROE, HARRIET, *Poets and Their Art* (New York: The Macmillan Co., 1926).

——————, *A Poet's Life* (New York: The Macmillan Co., 1938).

—————— and ALICE CORBIN HENDERSON, ed., *The New Poetry* (New York: The Macmillan Co., 1917; revised and enlarged, 1923, 1932; reprinted, 1925, 1926; reissued, 1926, 1927).

The New American Poetry, ed. Donald M. Allen (New York: Grove Press, Inc., 1960).

SMITH, WILLIAM JAY, *The Spectra Hoax* (Middletown: Wesleyan University, 1961).

STEAD, C. K., *The New Poetic* (London: Hutchinson, 1964).

THORP, N. HOWARD ("Jack"), in collaboration with Neil M. Clark, *Pardner of the Wind* (Caldwell: Caxton Printers, Ltd., 1945).

——————, *Songs of the Cowboys* (Estancia, New Mexico: News Print Shop, 1908; New York: enlarged edition with "Introduction" by Alice Corbin Henderson, Houghton Mifflin Co., 1921).

——————, *Songs of the Cowboys*, Variants, Commentary, Notes and Lexicon by Austin E. and Alta S. Fife; Music Editor Naunie Gardner (New York: Clarkson N. Potter, Inc., 1966).

UNTERMEYER, LOUIS, *Modern American and British Poetry* (New York: Harcourt, Brace and Co., 1922).

—————— and CARTER DAVIDSON, *Poetry, Its Appreciation and Enjoyment* (New York: Harcourt, Brace and Co., 1934).

VAN STONE, MARY R., *Spanish Folk Songs of New Mexico*, with a "Foreword" by Alice Corbin (Chicago: Ralph Fletcher Seymour, 1928).

WEST, JOHN O., "Jack Thorp and John Lomax: Oral or Written Transmission?" *Western Folklore*, XXVI (October 1967), 113-18.

WORDSWORTH, WILLIAM, "Preface" to Second Edition of *Lyrical Ballads* (1800), in George Saintsbury's *Loci Critici* (New York: Ginn and Co., 1903).

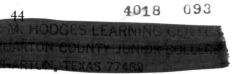